Surveillance society

ISSUES IN SOCIETY
Series Editor: Tim May

Current and forthcoming titles

Zygmunt Bauman: *Work, Consumerism and the New Poor*
David Byrne: *Social Exclusion*
Graham Crow: *Social Solidarities*
Mitchell Dean: *Governing Societies*
Gerard Delanty: *Citizenship in a Global Age*
Steve Fuller: *The Governance of Science*
Les Johnston: *Crime, Justice and Late Modernity*
David Knights and Darren McCabe: *Organizational Change*
Nick Lee: *Childhood and Society*
David Lyon: *Surveillance Society*
Graham Scambler: *Health and Social Change*
Piet Strydom: *Risk, Environment and Society*